Howdy!

Hillbilly Sayings and Redneck Humor

Collected, Edited and Illustrated by

John Leslie Oliver

Deep Read Press

www.deepreadpress.com

LAFAYETTE, TENNESSEE
deepreadpress@gmail.com

First Deep Read Press Edition

Manufactured in the United States of America

ISBN: 978-1-954989-54-2
Cover Image by John Leslie Oliver
Cover Design by Kim Gammon
Published by:
DEEP READ PRESS
Lafayette, Tennessee
www.deepreadpress.com
deepreadpress@gmail.com

What am a 'Hillbilly'?

"Let it be known rite here n rite now, being called a 'hillbilly' wuz a source of pride to him. He wuz independent, proud and livin' in these here hills wuz where he wanted to be!"

Cousin Rufus
(his epitaph, 1905)

In case you hadn't noticed, you can make a feller mad or you can be givin' them a compliment if you call them a 'hillbilly'.

The origins of that name am a little vague.

The people what lived in old Scotland used to call their hill dwellin' neighbors 'hill folks'. And, their word 'billy' wuz what they called a friend or companion.

It am likely that the descendants of the Scots n Irish people who settled in the hills of Appalachia used the word 'hillbilly' to refer to themselves.

The first use of 'hillbilly' in print wuz in 1892. A few years later, in 1900, a New York paper done wrote, "...a Hill-Billie is a free and untrammeled white citizen of Alabama, who lives in the hills, has no means to speak of, dresses as he can, talks as he pleases, drinks whiskey when he gets it, and fires off his revolver as the fancy takes him."

If you wuz to add a little fiddle music and the twang of the banjo and, oh yes, tossed in the makin' of whiskey, then that thar definition holds up even today!

We can't all be hillbillies!

The hills of Alabama that thar New York newspaper wuz referrin' to is at the far western end of the Appalachian mountain range, what starts in Canada and goes down the east coast of the good ole' US of A, and inter Alabama.

Them Yankee hill people don't think of themselves as being hillbillies and it ain't till you gets to Tennessee and Kentucky that we picks up that name n wears it with pride.

Sum of our cousins in the Missouri Ozarks call themselves 'hillbilly' n we let them cuz we don't blam 'em fer takin' pride in that thar distinction.

We advise you who ain't lucky nuff to be born n raised in the hills to use the word carefully, and if'n you do call someone a 'danged ole' hillbilly', be shore you foller that by sayin' "and, I'm glad to shake your hand, Cousin!"

Map of this here U S of A

end of the roaders

bogtrotters

rascals

flatlanders

Yankees

scalawags

river rats

ridgerunners

Hillbillies

squatters

trailer trash

rednecks

Sooners

clayeaters

crackers

porch monkeys

swamp people

briar hoppers

Lowdowners

sand bugs

They call it that "good ole mountain dew"

Why is it that hill folks n country people have such a fondness fer their homemade brew...moonshine?

It all goes back a long time ago, when the church run monasteries of Europe brewed beer, aged wine and distilled whiskey.

The monks then taught the native peoples of old Scotland and Ireland their craft and it didn't take long fer they wuz a makin' the beverage themselves.

The word 'whiskey' is Irish for 'the water of life."

But, it wuz the Scots who give us the word 'moonshine'.

Whether fer personal use or to sell, whiskey wuz a valuable commodity, so valuable that the King of England tried to tax it.

Well, ain't nobody likes paying taxes!

The Scottish whiskey brewers took to distillin' their brew after dark, so that the tax collectors couldn't see the smoke from the fire need to heat the mash.

They worked by the light of the moon, hence our word, 'moonshine'.

The King of England encouraged those troublesome Scots to move to Ireland, where with time, a new people evolved, the Scots-Irish.

In the 1700's, large numbers of them Scots-Irish immigrated to North America in pursuit of a better life.

But, them English settlers had beat them here.

So, the new arrivals wuz forced to move on down the coast of New England and into the mountains of Appalachia.

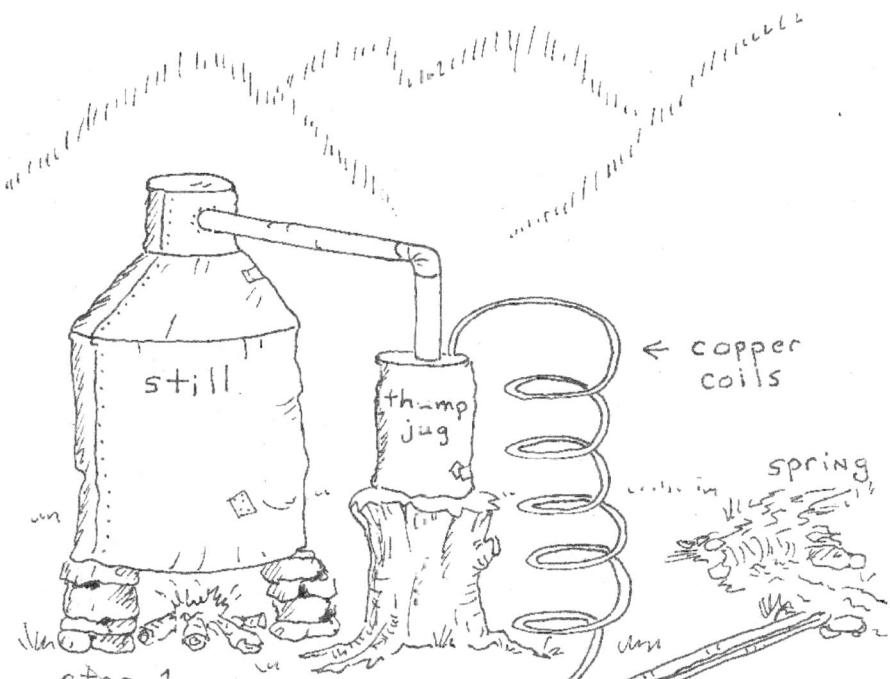

still

thump jug

← copper coils

spring

worm box

step 1
put the corn mash in the still n heat it

step 2
steam goes into the thump jug

step 3
the heated liquid is forced into the copper coils

step 4
spring water cools the copper coils n whiskey drips outta the worm box

xxx

9

Once thar, they found the cold clear waters of mountain springs were ideal fer makin' whiskey.

Now, in the old country the Scots-Irish used barley n rye, both of them bein' grains, to make the mash fer thar stills. In the mountains the Scot-Irish quickly larned to use the Native American corn to make thar mash...which is why we sumtimes call it 'corn liquor'.

When we gained our independence frum old England, it wuz our own American Guvernment what wanted to tax this potent liquid ... so, hill folks took to making it by the light of the moon agin! And, the tax collectors we call 'revenuers' cuz they is seeking 'revenue' for the government.

But, thar are other names fer moonshine:

white mule,

who shot Sally, corn licker,

two cats fightin', firewater, hooch,

mule kick, swamp root, boot leg,

rot gut, Kentucky hug, white lighting,

corn squeezins,

and 'mountain dew'!

Hillbilly Dialect

Every section of this here great land of ours has its own way of talkin', that is, of how they goes about pronouncing their wurds. The below wurds am spelled the way we hillbillies say 'em, so you will know how to talk proper when we and you is havin' a conversation:

wares – where is
>Wares that feller run off to?

tar – it takes four of 'em to make a car go
>I run over a nail and now I have a flat tar.

rotten pepper – stationary
>Give me sum rotten pepper so I can write to my congressman.

stow – place of business
>I done bought me sum boots at the shoe stow.

thank – to use your head
>I thank I needs to go to bed early tonight.

shivalay – not a Ford nor a Buick
>My rich uncle dun bought himself a new shivalay.

rassle – to grab a feller n throw him to the ground
>Thars gonna be a rasselin' match in town on Satiday.

mow – the opposite of less
>I needs sum mow of Ma's hot biscuits.

all – whut a automobile needs besides gas
>Check the all in my car, Rufus.

rite cheer – a definite place
>Sit down rite cheer n visit with us.

dawg – it ain't a cat
        My dawg dun chased a pole cat and now he stinks!

dock – when all the lights is out
        Boy, it shore am dock out tonight.

naw – when you'uns is answerin' in the negative
        Naw, I don't want no more grits on my plate.

aigs – they ain't shore which one come first
        Scramble us'uns sum aigs fer breakfast, Maw.

yo – when it belongs to you'un
        You can take yo business somewares else!

tail – to verbalize
        Don't tail me yo ain't got no money.

Clock – the furst name of that thar actor
        Mr. Clock Gable wuz in the movies.

auf – if it ain't on
        Tell Grampa to turn awf the radio so's we kin git sum sleep.

dreckly - purt soon
        You go on to the barn dance; I'll be thar dreckly.

far – what keeps you warm at night
        Put another log on the far, hit's cold in har!

mayan – when it ain't the missus
        That thar mayan works fer the government.

jist – a word preceding 'about'
        Sissie is jist 'bout done with sewin' up Pa's britches.

Watch your language, Paw!

Cuz most hill folks and country people also go to church regularly, they know the Lord's commandment against strong language. So, what can a feller say when they loses their temper?

Try a few of these on fer size:

Dag-nabbit!

Good Gravy!

Well, I'll be a monkey's uncle!

Dad-gummit!

For Pete's Sake!

What in tarnation?

What in the Sam Hill?

Son of a biscuit eater!

Gosh, almighty!

Lordy, Lordy, Lordy!

Jumpin' Jehoshaphat!

Good golly, Miss Molly!

Well, it that don't beat all?

Fiddle-de-dee!

Ah, baloney!

Go ask Moses!

When Granny Cooks

Cookin' over a hot cast iron stove required a lot of skill and a heap of know how.

Our granny never burned a pan of biscuits or made a bad batch of molasses cookies. Her secret to success may have been she knowed how to measure them thar ingrediants!

A 'smidgen' is just a 'teenie little bit'

3 'smidgens' makes one 'pinch'

4 'pinches' equals a 'spoonful'

2 'spoonfuls' give you a 'midlin' amount

3 'midlin' amounts makes one 'rite smart'

And it takes 5 'rite smarts' to make a 'whole heap'

We don't recall ever seein' Granny with a measuring cup!

What's fer supper, Granny?

Country folks know how to cook n how to eat, if'n it's a 'pot-luck' down at the reunion, a 'dinner on the grounds' after church, a 'box super' at the school house or a good ole' 4th of July picnic.

These here be some good ole' country eatin':

shucky beans
poke sallet
chess pie
corn puddin'
beans n taters
half moon pies
corn bread
cat's head biscuits
sweet taters
chicken gizzards
chitterlings
hog jowl
country ham
souse
dressin'
catfish
head cheese
hush puppies
blackberry cobbler
baloney n crackers

sweet tea
Moon Pies
sow belly
grits
watermelon
jerky
pork sausage
coke
hoppin' John
possum
hominy
sawmill gravy
lima beans
deviled eggs
bacon
pecan pie
sorghum molasses
Goo Goo candy bars
butter milk
pound cake

Granny's Buttermilk Biscuits

It warn't be rite fer us to be a talkin' 'bout biscuits and not give y'all the recipe, now would it.

Well, we reckon not, so here's the directions:

Granny would start by heatin' up the stove till when she placed her hand in the oven, the hair on her arm started to singe. But, if'n you ain't got a wood burnin' cast iron stove, you kin turn yore electric stove to 450 degrees.

You will be needin' 2 cups of self-rising flour
5 tablespoons of butter
A pitcher of buttermilk
1/4th teaspoon of soda

Cut the butter into the flour by hand...the way granny does, then you add the soda and a little buttermilk at a time till it makes a soft dough you can handle. Knead it a minute, not no more than a minute! Turn it out onto a floured board and roll it out to rite near one inch high. Now, use your biscuit cutter...Granny uses a jelly glass. But, now don't you go and twist that thar cutter. Lift it straight up from the dough. Lay them biscuits into the pan and pop 'em into the stove, till the tops be lightly brown. Now, get you sum more butter or fresh strawberry preserves and git to eatin'!

Ever thang but the "oink"!

Sausage, ham, bacon, pork chops, spare ribs, sow belly, pickled pig's feet, pork barbeque...the list goes on n on cuz we hillbillies love our pigs!

Thar's a reason hill folks rely on the pig fer breakfast, lunch and supper!

You see, in the day of the pioneers, thar warn't no way to have a beef cow and preserve its meat cuz the dang refrigerator hadn't been invented yet!

Ever farm had a milk cow and a yoke of oxen, but they didn't raise cattle fer eatin'. If'n you butchered a steer, you had best be prepared to eat the whole critter 'fore the day wuz over.

But, the lowely pig wuz our friend cuz we could salt the meat and hang it in the smoke house, smoke it and it would keep all winter.

That weren't no exaggeration when we hill people say, "We ate ever thang but the 'oink' !"

And, they wuz cheap to feed!

A hog could eat most anything...you've heerd of 'pig slop'. Well, that's kitchen scraps n rotten fruit n bad vegetables n whatever else a farmer could throw in thar, n' a pig would eat it with gusto! You could let a pig loose in the woods n they could fend fer themselves by eatin' nuts, roots, bugs, even lizards n snakes!

That explains our love affair with the pig.

I'll take a barbeque sandwich over a hamburger any ole day!

Words Country Folks be a usin'

We hillbillies, country folk n rednecks has our own language n folks frum elsewhar mite not understand it, so here's a little example of what we mean when we'uns use our special vocabulary:

rip snorter – big n powerful
> That thar wind wus a rip snorter!

jasper – a local character, lazy or meddlesome
> Some jasper came by the house sellin' vacuum cleaners.

poke – a sack or bag
> Put that 'possum in a poke fer me.

nubbin – a short person
> My pappy was a nubbin of a feller.

cattywumpus – twisted out of shape
> Granny's front porch is all cattywumpus.

piddle – to take yore time a doin' something
> Fetch this here letter to the mailbox, n don't you piddle.

alley apples – rocks found in a town alley way
> Let's grab sum alley apples and toss 'em at that ole' hound.

backer – a shortened version of 'terbacker'
> I'm old enuff to chaw backer and to spit it cross the room.

taters – the main part of most poor folks' supper
> Give me another helpin' of meat n taters, Maw!

a hoop and a holler – a measure of distance
> Aunt Letty lives a hoop and a holler frum here.

chigger – a purt near invisible critter that will up n bite you n you'ins will itch fer a week
Fer you go blackberry pickin', put sum coal oil on yore legs to keep them chiggers from a bitin'!

hissy fit – to lose yore temper, especially if'n you be a female
Maw had a hissy fit when she saw Paw talkin' to the Widow Jones after church last Go-to-meetin' day.

tuckered – to be tired or worn out
After plowin' all day, Bubba wuz tuckered out.

pester – to bother someone
Teacher! Johnny is a pesterin' me...make him stop!

wirty-durd – words not fit to be used in front of the preacher
Goober got in trouble fer usin' a wirty-durd in church.

sho-nuff – for real
That gal Judy is sho-nuff purty.

waller – to roll around in
Them pigs is happy to waller around in the mud.

that thar – to be specific
That thar feller is frum New Orleans.

this here – just as specific
Spencer, take this here apple to Miz Sallie, yore teacher.

addle – to pester
Jack, don't you addle me no more fer I gets mad.

vittles – food, grub...what you be a eatin'
I don't know what maw is a fixin' fer supper, but them vittles sho do smell good whiles they be a cookin'.

holler – a valley twix two hills
Uncle Ferd and Aunt Sissie live up in the holler.

yonder – sum distance frum here
   Violet's beau is frum over yonder ways.

chin music – jes plain ole' talkin'
   Luke n Cousin Liza wuz a sittin' on the porch swing jes a
   listenin' to each other's chin music.

bushel and a peck – a bunch n then a little more
   I told Miss Alice that I loved her a bushel and a peck!

goozle – a person's throat
   Grampa had the doctor to look down his goozle.

whipper-snapper – a kid what is full of themselves
   That young whipper-snapper, Jamison, dun run thru the
   house and out the door!

high falutin' – a person what thinks they is high society
   My cousin, Olivia, lives in one of them high falutin'
   neighborhoods of Nashville.

gussied up – puttin' on yore best britches or dress
   Aunt Emily and Uncle Dan wuz all gussied up fer the party.

ain't – another and more correct way of sayin' 'is not'
   Sheriff Blake says he ain't the one what shot the bank
   robber, hit wuz his deputy what dun it.

sorry – to make someone regret somethin' they dun
   If that feller kicks my dog again, I'll sorry him good!

dinner on the grounds – lunch after church, like a picnic
   Fer this Sunday's dinner on the grounds, Aunt Elizabeth is
   gonna make fried chicken and deviled eggs.

Yankee – a person frum north of the Mason Dixon line, what has
   overstayed thar welcome
   Our new neighbor is one of them dadblamed Yankees!

Kissin' Cousins

We talk 'bout our 'kissin' cousins' here in the hills...what we mean is a cousin that is close to us, close 'nuff by blood, that we kin jest walk rite up to 'em and kiss 'em!

Folks mite git confused when we talk 'bout a 'first cousin' or a 'second cousin, once removed' so here am an explanation:

Fer Starters,

- If'n your gramma or grampa had brothers or sisters, they be yore:
  Great Aunts n Great Uncles
- If'n yore maw or paw has brothers or sisters, then they be yore:
  Aunts n Uncles
- If'n yore aunts and uncles have children, they be yore"
  First cousins
- If'n yore first cousins have young'uns, they be yore:
  First cousins, once removed
- If'n you have kids, then yore kids and yore first cousin's kids will be:
  Second cousins to each other

Now, it stands to reason, if yore gramma died n yore gampa married again to a lady named Sue who wuz half his age, and if'n he up and died and you wuz to think Sue wuz rite purty n you married her – you would be yore own gampa!

Hit's been known to happen!

Penobscot
Delaware
Powhatan
Tuscarora
Catawba
Cherokee
Shawnee
Muskogee
Creek
Choctaw
Chickasaw
Tuskegee
Susquehana

Before Columbus

Long before that thar Columbus feller stumbled onto America, the First Peoples, or Native Americans, wuz livin' in these here mountains. Tribes such as the Cherokee, Shawnee, Powhatan, Lenape, Creek, Choctaw, Osage, Natchez and Iroquois made their home in the hills.

They left their mark on the land, not with buildings nor highways, but with place names that we still use nowadays.

These states wuz all named frum the languages of the First Peoples ... sum folks still call 'em 'Injuns'.

Massachusetts – the Algonquian people's word for "at the great hill."

Connecticut - comes from the Native American words for "beside the long tidal river".

Tennessee – is named for a Cherokee village, its meaning is uncertain.

Kentucky – from 'Kentake", an Iroquois word meaning 'meadow land'.

Mississippi – in the Ojibwe language, this means 'father of waters'.

Alabama – from two Choctaw words, 'alba' and 'amo', combined to describe the Choctaw practice of clearing land.

Some other place names: Paducah, Ky; Alleghany, NC; Kiawai Island, SC; Chattahoochee River, GA; Talladega, AL; and Chattanooga, TN.

Them ain't the only words that we got from the First Peoples. Here am some more: skunk, raccoon, coyote, moose, opossum, chipmunk, bayou, kayak, barbeque, squash, pecan, succotash, hickory, persimmon, shack, appaloosa and cannibal!

By the Light of the Moon

There be twelve cycles of the moon in a year. It takes a little over 29 days fer a moon to go frum full to completely dark to full again. That cycle is how the Native Americans kept up with the passin' of a year.

These are the twelve moons the Cherokee recognized n each moon held a special meaning:

- the Cold Moon – the 1st moon of the year, it coincides with the appearance of Venus in the sky, it am cold outside (Jan)
- the Bone Moon – the time in winter when food am scarce n bone marrow soup is 'bout all thar is to eat (Feb)
- the Windy Moon – when the 1st winds of spring blow (March)
- the Flower Moon – this is when the wild flowers start to bloom (April)
- the Plantin' Moon – time fer plantin' the 'three sisters', they bein' corn, beans and squash (May)
- the Green Corn Moon – the corn is green n it will show its tassel (June)
- the Ripe Corn Moon – you can now harvest the corn and roast them ears (July)
- the Fruit Moon – now is when the fruit trees are ripe (August)
- the Nut Moon – them trees what bear nuts will be droppin' em (September)
- the Harvest Moon – time fer celebratin' the harvest (Oct)
- the Trading Moon – this was when the tribes would visit each other and do a little tradin' (Nov)
- the Snow Moon – the traditional time fer snow to start fallin' (Dec)

Call me anything but 'late fer supper'

All of us-ins in the hills has names. Why sometimes we be the third generation to have the same name. We iz named fer our grandparents, fer generals in the War between the States, fer presidents, fer race car drivers n fer the weather!

But, it don't matter what yore folks call you, cuz hit don't take long fer you to have a 'nickname' and that's what'll be on yore tombstone!

Sum good ole' country boy nicknames:

Rooster, Hubcap, Bubba, Moose, Skinny, Spud, Preacher, Fats, Slick, Pops, Bud, Tinker, Rat, Stretch, Booger, Slim, Weezer, Red, Goober, Hoss, Muley, Gator, Jack Rabbit, Peewee, Catfish, Cooter and June Bug.

Sum good ole' country gal nicknames:

Sweetie Pie, Tadpole, Pumpkin, Tater Tot, Rosie, Squirt, Gertie, Little Bit, Sissie, Red, Pipsqueak, Sassy, Peanut, Cricket, Skeeter, Bee Bop, Ginger, Lizzie, Honey, Little Britches, Kitty, Sugar Pie, Stormy, Daisie Mae and Sunshine.

Give that dawg a bone!

Nearly every hillbilly has a dog, pronounced 'dawg'. It might be a coon hound or a bulldog or it might be a 'sooner'. A 'sooner' is "as soon this as it is that". My paw's dog wuz a 'Heinz 57' cuz Paw figured he was at least 57 varieties all rolled up into one!

We hillbillies use a lot of 'man's best friend' in our a talkin':

Pretty as a speckled pup in a red wagon.

He's a hard dog to keep under the porch.

Shakin' like a hound dog with a tick in his ear.

Havin' a wet dog in the house ain't the only way to
tell if it's a rainin'.

Happier than a dog with two tails.

I've got more problems than a run over dog.

He's puttin' on the dog.

Meaner than a junk yard dog.

He's barkin' up the wrong tree.

Here be sum good old country names fer a dog:

Yonder, Sparky, Rascal, Red, Cody, Blackie,
Bowser, Missie, Tug, Pip, Molly, Poochie,
Gator, Sweet Pea, Tank, Finn, Peaches,
Dawson, Bear, Ranger, Ruby, Prissy, Boy,
Buzzard, Scarlett, Cooper, Rocky and Brody

Here kitty, kitty

In the country, every farm had cats, but they wuz what we call 'barn cats' becuz 'litterboxes' were unheard of in the past. You wouldn't have a 'house cat'. Cats in the barn kept the mouse population under control. Oh, a cat might sit on the porch or sneak into the kitchen, but they knowed to sleep in the hay loft on a cold night.

Like dogs, cats am a part of our speech makin':

Faster than a dead cat can wag its tail.

He's tough, made of cat gut and baling wire.

Busier than a one eyed cat watchin' two rat holes.

As nervous as a long tailed cat in a room full of rockin' chairs.

Thar's not enuff room in that house to swing a dead cat.

There's more than one way to skin a cat.

I don't know where in the cat's hair it is.

Busy as a one legged cat in a sandbox.

Here be sum good old country names for yore cat:

Buzz, Sugar, Elvis, Missy, Belle, Dolly, Boo,
Sam, Lady, Princess, Ebony, Cocoa, Tiger,
Fuzzy Butt, Smoke, Angel, Snickers, Penny,
Dixie, Ginny, Pepper, Buttercup, Soda Pop,
Cookie, Babe, Ozzy, Lucky, Biscuit and Cookie.

Maybe you're a 'redneck'!

What's the difference between a hillbilly n a redneck?
I'll tell ya!

You can't be a 'hillbilly' lessen you live in hill country, hills so steep that the cows have legs on one side longer than they is on the other.

But, you kin be a 'redneck' and live just 'bout anywhere, tho you mite be partial to trailer parks.

If'n you works outdoors n the back of yore neck gits sunburned, you are a redneck fer shore!

Here's sum other ways to recognize a redneck:

- Yore idea of 'dressin' up' is to wear a clean tee shirt.
- When yore name is in the local newspaper, it's under the Police Report and it ain't cuz you were the arrestin' officer.
- If your house catches on fire, you grab the kids with one hand n yore big screen TV with the other. Don't worry, yore wife is rite behind you with the baby and her prom dress.
- The back of your truck has more empty beer cans than tools.
- Yore bathroom is ten feet behind the house.
- The only flower in yore yard is Kudzu.
- Yore wife dresses to match yore tattoos.
- At the restaurant you ask the waitress what type of salad dressin' they have besides Ranch and after she lists them you say, "I'll have Ranch."
- You tell the doctor, "The last thing I remember is me sayin', "Hey, Yall, watch this!"
- Yore wife can spell her name three ways n you have it misspelled on your chest.
- You spray paint yore girlfriend's name on the town water tank.
- If yore mama ain't happy, ain't nobody happy.

There's No Place Like Home

We hill folks am proud of our hometowns n we git homesick rite easy if'n we go to a town big enuff to have stoplights. Them big city folks say, 'War you frum?" n we tell 'em with pride whar we is frum. And, we mite be frum one of these here unique places:

Tennessee:

Bean Station
Big Sandy
Bugtussle
Ducktown
Jasper
Jellico
Moscow
Niota
Red Boiling Springs
Soddy-Daisy

Virginia

Big Rock
Bridgewater
Chantilly
Horse Pasture
Lightfoot
Ripplemead
Sleepy Hollow
Triangle
Wicomico
Tookland

West Virginia:

Big Chimney
Chester
Hico
Hometown
Jolo
Man
Nutter Fort
Paw Paw
Red Jacket
Tornado

Louisiana:

Boglausa
Cut Off
Hackberry
Manou
Many
Moss Bluff
Olla
Samtown
Tickfaw
Waterproff

Alabama

Moody
Arab
Boaz
Clayhatchee
Double Springs
Eutaw
Green Pond
Pea Ridge
Good Hope
Tallapoosa

Kentucky

Avawam
Beaver
Cave City
Dry Ridge
Flat Lick
Gamaliel
Horse Cave
Mousie
Rabbit Hash
Sunshine

Georgia

Alamo
Cedartown
Chicopee
Coffee
Dunwoody
Five Forks
Hephzibah
Panthersville
Pooler
Sugar Hill

Mississippi

Belzoni
Bogue Chitto
Cold Water
Jumpertown
Piney Woods
Scooba
Soso
Yazoo City
Beulah
Picayune

Preachin' n Baptizin'

Hillbillies am church goin, God fearin', foot stompin', singin' and praisin' glory folks. We take our religion seriously. We kain't begin to list the many faiths we'uns take to, but I kin tell you this. Each of us am convinced thar ain't no other way to our reward in the sky, 'cept thru our own particular faith!

Do I hear an 'amen'?

Tain't no surprise that we sprinkle our religion in our talkin.

Here be some examples:

About a nar-do-well:

That feller is shiftless, tried everthing but preachin'.

To mean a long time:

'from now till they git religion'

When confused about what to call the noon meal and the evening meal:

It wuz the 'Last Supper' not the "Last Dinner".

In recognizing a brave man:

Why, he wasn't afraid to charge into hell with a bucket of ice.

On profanity:

He could cuss in seven languages and four religions.

If a person wouldn't change their mind:

They're as stubborn as Balaam's ass.

Of a long suffering man is a difficult marriage:

Ole Clyde has the patience of Job.

To explain a graveyard ghost:

I reckon the devil wouldn't take 'em and the Lord didn't want 'em.

When asked why every town, big or small, has its share of sinnin':

For where God built a church, there the devil built a chapel.

On a really hot day:
    I swear, it must be hotter than the devil's pepper patch.

A comment on being hungry:
    An empty stomach makes for a short grace.

Explaining a woman who is always in a bad mood:
    She must a been baptized in prune juice.

To encourage a person to get to work:
    God helps those who help themselves.

The reason folks put their sons to plowin' at an early age:
    An idle mind is the devil's playground.

The "A-men Corner"

You may have heard of someone sittin' in the A-men Corner. If'n you are confused as to where that is, here's an explanation:

In the old days, men and women sat on opposite sides in the church sanctuary.

In some churches, they also entered thru separate doors.

It wuz always, women to the right and men to the left.

Once inside, the same was true for where they was to sit, women on the right and men on the left. That put the men facing the preacher at the pulpit cuz the pulpit would be on the left to allow room for the choir, which always sat on the right.

Sometimes an old feller sittin' down in front of the preacher would git caught up in the sermon and shout, "Amen, Brother!", which meant that he agreed with what the preacher had said.

That side of the aisle became known as the "A-men corner."

Sayin' Grace

You never know when the preacher will holler out over the congregation and say, "Brother Alfonzo, will you give us a prayer?" Most folks knows at least one short prayer to say fer most occasions.

Here be sum you mite wanna memorize jes in case you am the one called upon!

A partin' prayer: May your neighbors respect you,
                        Trouble neglect you,
                    The angels protect you,
                        N heaven accept you, ... Amen

At a meal: Lord, we thank you,
                    For the food before us,
                    The friends beside us,
                    The love between us,
                    N your presence among us, ... Amen

At a funeral: Lord, we thank you,
                    For givin' us this soul,
                    For the years we shared with 'em,
                    For the laughter n the tears,
                    May you hold 'em close to your heart,
                    That we will know where to find 'em,
                    When we make our own journey.
                    Thy will be done, ... Amen

Sing ye brothers n sisters, sing!

Tain't nothin' like goin' to a church tent revival and hearin' the 'good word'. But what gets the crowd standing is a good ole' hymn led by the song leader with everyone thar filled with the 'spirit'.

These be some of our favorites:

Amazing Grace
Blessed Assurance
Come sinners, to the gospel feast
Go Down, Moses
Go, tell it on the mountain
How Great Thou Art
I come to the garden alone
I heard an old, old story
Lift every voice and sing
Marching to Zion
My hope is built on nothing less
Nothing but the blood of Jesus
Old Rugged Cross
On Jordon's stormy banks I stand
Rescue the perishing
Rock of Ages
Shall we gather by the river
Stand up, stand up for Jesus
Swing low, sweet chariot
There is a balm in Gilead
This little light of mine
'Tis so sweet to trust in Jesus
What can wash away my sins?
When we all get to heaven

The Little House Out Back

You don't have to be half smart to know that ever hillbilly home has a 'little house out back'...you might even call it the 'outhouse' or 'privy', short for the private place to care of business.

They kin be simple or fancy. Old George Washington had his privy built outta brick n it even had windows!

Fore they invented 'indoor plumbing', everbody had an outhouse. If'n you had a big family you mite have a 'two holer', a regular size hole fer the adults and a smaller one fer the children.

The ole one room school would have two...one fer the girls n one fer the boys.

If you wuz to stay at a hotel in them days, they would mark the door of the ladies' outhouse with a half moon, so they'd know which one wuz fer them. The mens' outhouses would have a star on the door.

Most outhouses didn't have nuthin' on their doors cuz it wuz fer everbody in the family anyhows.

In the old days people didn't have toilet paper so they used leaves, moss, corncobs, n such. When Mr. Sears n Mr. Roebuck come out with thar catalogue, well it soon had another purpose!

You had to be carful 'bout goin' to the outhouse in the dark cuz on Halloween, it wuz a prank to move the family privy back five feet, so that if'n you wuz to go take a wiz after dark, you might end up in the hole! One year, Gramps moved the family privy back five feet 'fore the hooligans arrived to play thar trick, n it wuz them what ended up in the hole!

Them good ole' days am gone now that we got plumbin' in the house.

Young folks today will never know the excitement of sittin' in an outhouse on a cold January mornin'!

Redneck Weatherman

We'uns don't need no fancy television weatherperson to tell us what the durn weather is cuz all we'uns gots to do is nail a piece of rope by the back door n we kin tell the weather jes like our great grand-pappy done!

If'n the rope is wet – it's a rainin'

If'n the rope is movin' – thar's a wind a blowin'

If'n the rope is hot – the sun am a shinnin'

If'n the rope is cool – it's rite cloudy

If'n the rope is stiff – it's a mite cold outside

If'n the rope is white – why, it's a snowin'

If'n the rope is gone – run fer the hills, it's a tornado!

The 12 Seasons of Appalachia

Most parts of this here country of ours has four seasons: summer, fall, winter and spring. But, in the hills n hollers of these mountains, we'uns is blessed to have twelve:

Winter

false hope fer spring

second winter

maybe spring

jes kiddin' – winter again

pollen spring

actual spring

summer

field trip to the sun

false fall

summer again

actual fall

As we tell folks who visit here, "If'n you don't like the weather, jes wait cuz it'll change fer the week's over!"

Varmits n Critters!

We hill people has to share the hills with a whole mess of God's creatures. Not all of 'em is fun to be around. Here am a list of some critters what you need to be careful around, cuz most all of 'em knows how to bite!

Chiggers
Pole cats (skunks)
Ticks
Snappin' turtles
Ground hogs
Waspers
Bed bugs
Muley calves
Bulls
Raccoons
Chicken snakes
Squirrels
Cave bats
Black racers
Dirt dabbers
Bears
Skeeters

How does a feller get to over thar from right here?

Uncle Cletus wuz a settin' on his porch one hot afternoon when a city slicker drove up in a big fancy black SUV.

"I need some directions!" he hollered to Uncle Cletus.

"Why, shore 'nuff...I'd be glad to help out", Uncle Cletus answered.

"Does this road go to Nashville?" the man said.

"Well, Mr. ... I've lived here all my life n I ain't never seen this road go nowhere. It jes stays put", Uncle said.

That city feller didn't look too happy with that answer so he snapped back at Uncle Cletus, "Tell me this...how do you get to Nashville?"

Uncle politely replied, "My boy Jesse takes me,"

Now, that city man was gittin' pretty agitated, and he says, "You lived here all your life, Old Man?"

"Not yet!" Uncle Cletus said.

That thar feller was gittin' red in the face by now n he says rite smart like, "You don't know much do you!"

"I know I ain't lost!" Uncle Cletus smiled back.

If'n you were to stop by a country house n ask fer directions, this here is a good guide to how long it mite take to 'git thar'.

Next door – 1 to 2 minutes
Rite up the road – 5 to 10 minutes
A couple of miles – 10 to 20 minutes
Not too far – 20 to 50 minutes
Just a little ways - over an hour
A purty good drive – 2 hours or more

Jes be glad that the person yore asking directions of don't say, "You can't git thar from here!"

Being Muley!

A mule is a dang shure hard workin' animal. Us hill folks prefer to work a team of mules over a yoke of oxen or a hitch of horses any ole' day.

It takes the couplin' of a jackass n a mare to make a mule n the offspring is an improvement over either of thar parents.

Them thar college people have tested 'em and showed that mules are better at problem solvin' than a dog, a donkey or a horse!

That thar is why folks call 'em' stubborn. A mule won't do nuthin' it thinks is dangerous or that it don't understand. You have to work with 'em to do a new task, but once you do they is hard workers.

One more thang I bet you didn't know...a mule knows when to quit. A mule won't let itself be overworked! They will jes stop what they are a doin'.

That's why we call some folks 'muley', cuz they are as stubborn as a mule!

My Paw used to say, 'Nowadays, don't nobody work hard 'cept a mule and he has to back up to it!"

Rite here's a story they tells on my third cousin' once removed, Slim.

Slim done traded his mule to Henry Perkins fer a suit of Sunday go to meeting clothes. A few days later, Henry seen Slim and he is fit to be tied. He hollers to Slim, "See here, Slim, why didn't you tell me that mule was lame before I bought him frum you?"

Slim looked rite sheepish n said, "Well, Henry, the feller what sold him to me didn't say nuthin' 'bout it, so I just thought it was a secret!"

Why you worthless #!@?*

When a hillbilly or a redneck gits aggravated, they can use a heap of adjectives to describe the jasper what made 'em mad.

The next time you find yoreself getting' a little aggravated, feel free to borrow sum of these here words:

no good

rotten

cheap

low life

snake lickin'

over stuffed

ignorant

brainless

bug eyed

fat assed

blood suckin'

heartless

four-flushin'

knuckle headed

halfwit

I'll bet you put that varmint in thar place!

And, don't let the bedbugs bite!

In the old days, folks didn't let nothin' go to waste. If'n a dress wore out, the buttons wuz cut off n used again. The scraps wuz used to mend the elbows and knees of shirts n britches. What wuz left over wuz put aside to piece together a patchwork quilt.

Twarn't no better sleep that that on a feather mattress, under a patchwork quilt, with the rain a tip-tappin' on a tin roof.

The squares of a patchwork quilt had designs what wuz worked out over the years. Here be sum of the names fer those purty patterns:

Star of Bethlehem
Garden of Eden
Old Maid's Puzzle
Hearts n Gizzards
Solomon's Temple
Wedding Knot
The Road to California
Friendship Quilt
Democrat Rose
Joseph's Coat
Drunkard's Path
Swinging Corners
Log Cabin
Sugar Loaf
Forbidden Fruit Tree
Lincoln's Platform
Tree of Paradise

Shave n a haircut...two bits!

Many hillbillies have a beard n wears it with pride. This here is a guide to tell what kind of person it am by how long thar beard be:

caveman – ain't shaved fer a week

manley – a goatee

Amish – long chin whiskers

trucker – bushy from ear to ear

hippie – long with a few flowers here n thar

biker – covers his chest tattoos

hillbilly – can be tucked into his overalls

lumberjack – resembles Paul Bunyan

professor – long and neatly trimmed

wizard – white and reaches to his waist

God – purt near touchin' His toes!

Country Lawyers

The men n women what study the law is important to the lives of every country town, no matter how small.

A feller never knows when he might have to go before the judge to plead his case on why his pigs were in the neighbor's corn.

Aunt Ida wuz once called to testify, down at the county courthouse, cuz she wuz a witness to a crime.

The defendant's lawyer didn't believe her testimony that his client, Moses Shagnasty had stole a watermelon from the patch of her neighbor, Charlie Presley.
"I see'd him with my own eyes," Aunt Ida said.
"How fer away were you, Aunt Ida, weren't you standin' in your backyard by the outhouse?," the lawyer asked.
"Sho' nuff", Aunt Ida replied, "and I see'd Moses pick up that watermelon and toss in the back of his wagon."
"That's a mighty long way...from yore backyard, next to yore outhouse, to Charlie's watermelon patch! Are you shure you kin see that far?" that lawyer sneered.
"Yes, I'm shure I kin see that far, " Aunt Ida snapped rite back.
Convinced that Aunt Ida couldn't have recognized Moses from that distance, the lawyer said rite loud fer the whole courtroom to hear, "Well, Aunt Ida, jest tell us...how fer can you see?"
"I kin see the moon!", she said as loud as she could!
And that wuz that!
The judge found Moses guilty and sentenced him to one week's hard labor on the county roads!

Banjoes n Fried Okra !

African Americans have had a big influence on the culture n music of the hills.

While it am true that most black folks come to the mountains as slaves, it am a fact that it wuz the flat land people what had cotton n tobacco and sugar cane plantations what most used slave labor.

Once here, black Americans put their stamp on hillbilly ways.

The seeds fer watermelon, black-eyed peas, sorghum n okra come over from Africa on the slave ships and so did the very first banjos on these shores.

It wuz a black cook what throwed a piece of chicken into a pan of hot lard n first served fried chicken!

The same can be said fer fried catfish, fried okra and potato chips!

It am likely that hush puppies owe their origin to a black cook.

We'uns owe a lot to our African American neighbors.

Whar would Bluegrass music be if'n it warn't fer the banjo. Gospel music got a lot of its 'soul' from African American spirituals. And, we ain't gonna fergit Rhythm n Blues or Hip Hop music.

So, the next time you all be' a sittin' down to a Sunday dinner of fried chicken, or you is out on the floor dancing to some lively banjo tunes, jes be rememberin' the contributions of black Americans to our country.

Turn the Radio on!

Nashville, Tennessee, is called 'Music City', USA cuz of its long association with country music, and that thar Grand Ole' Opry.

Hill folks would sit n listen to the radio ever Saturday nite to hear such great songs as 'I'm so lonesome I could cry", "The Walbash Cannonball", and "I'm walkin' the floor over you."

Not every song what gits written makes it to the hit parade. Here am some songs that didn't make it. We wonder why:

If the Jukebox Took Teardrops, I'd Cry All Night Long
Black-eyed Peas and Blue-eyed Babies
You Hurt the Love Right Out of Me
She Made Toothpicks of the Timber of my Heart
Get Your Biscuits in the Oven and Your Buns in the Bed
You're the Reason Our Kids Are So Ugly
If Fingerprints Showed Up on Skin, Wonder Whose I'd Find on Yours
Katy Did and Dinah Might
Fly the Friendly Skies with Jesus
I'm the One She Missed Him with Tonight
If Whiskey Were A Woman, I'd Be Married for Sure
Next Time I Fall in Love, I Won't
I'm All He's Got, but He's Got All of Me
If I'd Shot Her When I Met Her, I'd Be Outta Jail by Now
I Saw Elvis in a UFO
I've Got the Hungrees for Your Love n I'm Waiting in Your Welfare Line

Your Cheatin' Heart
Causes of death in Country Music songs:

It am bad enuff fer a feller or a gal to die a tragic death, but then someone goes n writes a song 'bout it and then sings it on the radio. Since the days of Tom Dooley hangin' from a white oak tree, to today, we is still dyin' n singin' 'bout it.

These here be the seven main ways people in pushin' up daisies in country music songs:

1. – shot by yore lover – probably down by the river

2. - run over by a train – they'll have a funeral when all the pieces are found

3. – kicked in the head by a mule – that'll learn you to walk up behind one

4. – bad whiskey – must a been the dead skunk they pulled outta the mash

5. – shot in a game of cards – you had five aces, Son!

6. – of a broken heart – this mite involve a dog

7. – just up n died – when yore time is up, it's up!

He Ain't So Smart!

Thar's an old tale 'bout the foolish young feller what walked into the blacksmith shop and stood thar watchin' the man forge a new horse shoe. When the man laid the shoe on the anvil, the young feller moved closer to take a look, reachin' out his hand as if he wuz gonna pick it up. The blacksmith said, "Careful, Son, thats' hot!"

But, the kid wuz foolish and picked it up anyway. He quickly dropped it.

Burned yourself, didn't ya," the blacksmith said.

"Nope", the foolish kid answered, "It jes didn't take me long to look at it!"

Well, in the hills we have ways to describe those fools who pass our way:

-he couldn't break an egg if he stood on it.

-he's a brick shy of a load

-if brains were lard, he wouldn't have enuff to grease a skillet

-his phone is off the hook

-the porch light is on but nobody's home

-their cornbread ain't done in the middle

-he couldn't find his own hand in his own pocket

-he couldn't drive a nail thru a pumpkin

-when they handed out brains, he thought they said 'trains and said, "give me slow one"

The signs fer plantin'!

Them folks what farm fer a livin' know when to plant and when not to plant if'n they wants a good garden. Here be some particuars 'bout plantin' that all country folks knows:

-wait fer apple trees to bloom before plantin' your bush beans

-when the apple blossoms fall, it am safe to plant your pole beans n your cucumbers

-when your lilacs are in full bloom, you kin plant squashes

-when the bearded iris are bloomin', it is time to plant peppers n eggplants

-plant yore melons, such as cantaloupe, when peonies blossom

-sow yore morning glory seeds when the leaves on the maple tree are fully growed

-anything what grows below the ground, such as carrots or potatoes, should be planted during a waning moon (goin' from full to a quarter moon)

-foods what grow above the ground, such as tomatoes, corn or pumpkins, should be planted during a waxing moon (going from a moonless nite to a full moon)

-You can transfer yore tomato seedlin's to the garden when the lily of the valley is in full flower

Will You Be Mine?

Valentine's Day will git us hillbillies a buyin' candy n pickin' flowers down by the cemetery to give to our sweethearts. Here is some nice poems to say to that special somebody:

Pigs love pumpkins,
Cows love squash,
Who loves you?
I do by gosh!

As sure as the grass,
grows 'round the stump,
You are my darlin'
Sugar Lump!

A kiss is a germ,
Or, so it's been stated,
But, kiss me quick,
I've been vaccinated!

I love you, I love you.
I love you so well,
If I had a peanut,
I'd give you the shell!

Don't make out,
By the garden gate,
Love is blind,
 But, the neighbors aint'!

Ashes to ashes,
 Dust to dust,
 If we don't kiss,
Our lips will rust!

If I were a head of lettuce,
I'd cut myself in two,
I'd give the leaves to all my friends,
And, save the heart for you!

The ocean is wide,
 The sea is level,
Come to my arms,
 You little devil!

Am you a lucky fellow?

If'n you wuz to be born and raized in the country, then you know that thar are some thangs that are bad luck n some thangs that are good luck. Rite here we give you a list of both, so's you will be prepared.

It am bad luck to:

- break a mirror
- walk under a ladder
- lay yore hat on a bed
- have a black cat cross yore path
- close a pocket knife that someone else has done opened
- walk with one shoe on and one shoe off
- sing at the supper table
- build a new house on the foundation of one that has burned
- leave a house thru a different door than the one you entered
- sneeze at the breakfast table
- count the cars in a funeral procession
- have more than one person stir the cake batter
- move an old broom into a new house
- hear a rooster crow in the middle of the night
- count yore money in the middle of a poker game, before the game is over
- spill salt at the table
- step over a grave
- hear the church doors rattle during a sermon
- open an umbrella in the house
- to hang a horseshoe upside down

Jest like thar are thangs that are unlucky, thar be thangs that be lucky.

My little brother Buford was braggin' one day that he had a lucky rabbit's foot in his pocket.

Granny said, "Why Lordy, boy, that ain't lucky. That thar rabbit had four of 'em and look where it got him!"

These here be good luck to:
- find a four leaf clover
- find a penny with the heads side up
- blowout all the candles on a birthday cake with one blow
- for a butterfly to lite on yore shoulder
- spit on yore fish bait
- make a wish on the first night when you sleep in a new bed
- blow all the seeds of a dandelion off in one blow
- keep a rattlesnake's rattle inside yore fiddle
- find a horse shoe and to hang it on a wall with the open side up
- kiss a girl while leaning over a cow's back
- place a pillowcase on a double bed with the open end facing away from the bed, so nightmares can find their way out
- wish upon a star
- see a shooting star
- rub the back of someone who is hunchbacked
- for a bride to have with her, something old, something new, something borrowed and something blue
- catch a leaf as it falls from a tree
- have it snow on yore garden in March

Cold weather may be a coming!

Don't nobody in the hills looks forward to a cold winter nor a hot summer. We'uns try to predict what the weather will be...hot or cold, wet or dry...by takin' a look-see at nature.

Here be sum things we'uns swear by:

- when the wind is from the east, it's neither good fer man nor beast
- a hornet buildin' its nest close to the ground is a sure sign of a cold winter with lots of snow
- if'n a woollyworm's coat is more black than brown, winter will be cold.
- some folks say thar will be a snow fer every black stripe on that thar woollyworm's back
- count the fogs in August n you will know how many snows we'll git
- if acorns are plentiful in the fall, snow will be heavy in the winter
- dry grass in the mornin' means rain later in the day
- cows will lie down on the ground n stay thar if'n it's gonna rain
- birds fly low in the sky before a storm
- a sow (mama pig) will gather sticks n corn cobs to make a nest jest before a winter storm
- when the frogs in the pond won't stop croakin', it means rain
- count the seconds between a flash of lightning n hearin' the thunder, and fer every five seconds, the storm is a mile away
- when the moon wears a halo in winter, thar will be snow, n if'n the moon wears a halo in summer, thar will be rain
- if'n a muskrat builds its nest high on the creek bank, watch out fer a rainy winter with floodin'
- if'n the raccoons have thick tails, winter will be hard
- Grampa's knees will ache and give him pain jest before a storm

74

A bad spell of whether!

If you had a went to school in a one room log cabin, and only went when you weren't needed to help plow, you would be a bad speller too! These here be sum common wurds that we hill dwellers has truble spellin':

new monua
yeller skwash
dawg
geetar
Urope
zookeene
pair-a-shoot
peech
lukshurient
qcomebur
roebot
vegitible
stumick
rezurecshun
purty
alfabet
kumfurtable
egsactly
idyan
backwerd
flecksible
razzberry
hipopotimus
sourkraut
congrigashun
awtum
frekels
kitastrofy
instink

Poems to recite fer the teacher!

The next time yore teacher asks the class to learn a poem to recite fer the annual school May Day program, you jes mite find one of these here poems what will make yore parents proud of you!

Yonder comes Paw,
With a snicker n a grin,
Groundhog gravy,
All over his chin!

> Fishy, fishy in the brook,
> Daddy caught him with a hook,
> Mama fried him in the pan,
> Baby ate him like a man!

I wear my blue pajamas,
    In the summer when it's hot,
I wear my flannel nighties,
    In the winter when it's not,
And sometimes in the springtime,
    And sometimes in the fall,
I jump rite in between the sheets,
    With nothin' on at all!

> When paw goes fishin'
> With lures or with flies,
> The smaller the catch,
> The bigger the lies!

Mary had a little lamb,
She fed it castor oil,
Every time it jumped the fence,
It fertilized the soil!

Are you the one,
The mule kicked?
No sir, I'm the one,
The cow licked!

I've got a gal,
And a bulldog too,
My gal don't love me,
But, my bulldog do!

The moon shines east,
The moon shines west,
My grampa makes,
The moonshine best!

I stole them britches,
I also stole the corn,
But, twarn't no crime,
As sure as you're born,
If the motive is right,
Where's the sin,
I stole them britches,
To be baptized in!

June bug has a golden wing,
    Lighting bug has a flame,
Bedbug has no wings at all,
    But, he gits thar jes the same.

That Ole Persimmon Tree

(A purty poem fer you'uns to enjoy)
(by Johnny Whitson)

When I wuz a kid, nearly sixteen,
  My Pappy said to me,
"Let me tell you sumtin' 'bout,
  That ole' persimmon tree,

Persimmon tree ain't too purty,
  N' its fruit shore ain't sweet,
But, it will pucker up yore lips,
To kiss any ole' gal you meet!

I thought 'bout what Pappy said,
N' picked me a big ole' fruit,
I took a bite and boy howdy!
  It was impossible to chew it!

My face got all cross-eyed,
The fruit was sure sour loaded,
My nose turned a shade of red,
  My head purt near exploded!

My upper lip begun to curl,
  My bottom lip to quiver,
They puckered up together,
I started to shake and shiver,

Out of the corner of my eye,
  I seen a gal approachin',
She give me a "come here" look,
I didn't need no coachin'!

With my lips all puckered up,
I grabbed ahold n' kisser her!
She musta like what I done,
She said, "Do that again, Mister!"

Now, Saturday nites, I fill my pockets,
Not with oranges, apples or lemons,
I go to town lookin' fer gals,
  With my pockets full of persimmons!

Is yore belly achin'?

Thar warn't no need to call on the doctor when you wuz sick. All you'un had to do wuz to go to Granny n she would set you rite.

Here am some tried n true remedies, sho nuff!

-put a mixture of spider webs n sugar on a small cut or scratch
-spit some snuff or chewing tobacco juice on a bee sting
-make a poultice of turpentine n goose grease n put it on the chest of someone who has a cold n is havin' breathin' problems
-when you'un first gits a cold, drink a hot toddy of warm whiskey, lemon juice, ginger n honey
-fer a cough, take a spoonful of sugar mixed with a dose of turpentine
-when chiggers bite, n you haff to itch, put a dab of warm bacon grease on the bite
-make yore own cough syrup by lettin' a few pieces of hard candy dissolve in a little whiskey, then add a little honey
-keep a stolen potato in yore pocket to prevent boils
-sassafras tea drunk in the spring will prevent summer chills
-drinkin' sulfur water from a mineral spring am good fer digestion
-brown paper from a grocery bag, soaked in vinegar, placed on the forehead, am good for headaches n it am also good fer bruises
-wash yore face in stump water to remove freckles
-poison ivy will dry up if bathed in a mixture of gun powder n sweet milk
-if you mash yore big toe, go stick it in a warm pile of cow manure fer a few minits to prevent infection
- to git rid of a wart, cut an apple in half, rub the apple on the wart, then bury the apple in yore garden, guaranteed!

Gone fishin'!

Thar's no better way to spend a hot summer day than to go down to the pond or maybe the creek, n go fishin'. If'n you wuz frum hill country, then you'd know to dig yore worms in the cool of the evenin' after a big rain n you'd know that these air the fish you wants to catch:

small mouth bass
crappie
blue gill
large mouth bass
walleye
gar
catfish
sauger
drum
paddlefish

Uncle Clem wuz fishin with the preacher one day n they commenced to brag 'bout what all they had caught on that thar stretch of the river.

The preacher thought he'd out brag ole' Uncle Clem when he said he had once hooked a sixty pound channel catfish thar.

Uncle Clem huffed n said, "Why, that ain't nuthin', one day I throwed out my line and brung up an old radio somebody had thrown away and the radio wuz a still playin'.

The preacher looked at Uncle Clem n accused him of a lyin' n Uncle Clem said he hadn't never seen a channel catfish what weighted sixty pounds.

After sittin' in the boat fer a while, both of 'em a fummin', Uncle Clem said to the preacher, "If you'll take twenty pounds off that catfish, I'll turn that radio off!"

Tuff as woodpecker lips!

We country folks don't have no trouble talkin' trash 'bout our neighbors, or our kinfolk, why even on ourselves. We'uns always have a way of describin' a feller or some gal to someone what never met 'em before.

See rite here what I'm talkin' 'bout:

- he thought he wuz as tuff as woodpecker lips
- they had to tie a porkchop to his leg to git the dog to play with him
- she's as old as gully dirt
- that boys so skinny, the only thing holdin' his pants up is the starch
- you don't have to be a veterinarian to know a horses' patootie when you see one
- they're as common as pig's tracks
- he's so lazy, if you gave him a job sleepin', he'd wake up and quit
- why, he's faster than a sneeze thru a screen door
- he's so poor his shoelaces don't match
- they're eatin' ham on sowbelly wages
- he wuz so flabbergasted he could have fallen thru his butt hole and hung himself
- she wuz busier than a one-legged man at a butt kickin' contest
- they're frum a jack-rabbit neighborhood
- she's choppin high cotton
- he thought he wuz sexier than socks on a rooster
- -they looked like they had been rode hard and put up wet
- he wuz as weak as boardin' house coffee
- they're so thin they'd have to stand twice to make a shadow

Superstitions 'bout Death

Hill people has a lot of superstitions 'bout death n dyin'. Some of those beliefs come from the Scot-Irish, some be from Africa n some be from the Native Americans. Jes talkin' 'bout it makes me nervous.

Read what am written below rite careful n take the appropriate precautions n don't say we didn't warn you!

- a bird at the window, tryin' to git in is a sign that someone in the family is 'bout to die
- if a person's picture falls off from its place on the wall, it's a sign they has up and died
- when you carry a dead person out of the house or the funeral home, be sure to carry them out feet first or someone else in the house will follow 'em to the grave.
- if a red-headed woodpecker pecks on the side of your house, it is a drivin' nails into yore coffin
- when someone in the house dies, be quick to turn all the mirrors 'round backwards so their spirit won't see itself and git caught in the mirror and never leave
- stop all the clocks in the house if'n somebody dies, so the devil won't know they are dead and the deceased person's spirit kin git to heaven befor' the devil even knows they is gone
- if in yore dreams you see seven white horses, there will soon be a death in the family
- grass won't grow here a dead body had done lay on the ground
- if you wuz to cut off a piece of rope used to hang someone and you wuz to keep that piece of rope in yore pocket, it will protect you frum harm

Epitaphs

When we bury folks it's the proper thang to do to rite a verse onto the stone. These here am sum what mite make you ponder on the 'here after':

Here lies my wife,
    Here let her lie,
Now, she's at rest,
    And so am I!

            If I git to heaven,
            'fore you do,
            I'll make a hole,
            N pull you thru !

Death took
    His soul up,
Now, his body,
    Fills this hole up!

          Here lies an atheist,
          He makes a show,
          All dressed up,
          N no place to go !

Poem n epitaphs,
    Are but stuff,
Here I lie,
    N that's enuff !

        Here lies Bubba Cain,
        Always a wheelin' n a dealin',
        Now, this am where he lies,
        He got caught a chicken stealin'!

Sum tall tales!

Ain't nobody kin tell a whooper like my cousin Jethro. Here am sum of his best tall tales:

- That thar hail storm we had last week, beat holes in the ground deep enough to set fence posts.
- August wuz so dry here-a-bouts that the trees wuz chasin' dogs down the street
- I ain't sayin' it wuz hot, but the hens back at the barn wuz pickin' up worms with pot holders.
- I'll tell you how much rain we had last nite – I seen the catfish in the creek a climbin' trees.
- My neighbor wanted to hire a mover. I told him that with my truck I could move most anything. I told him I once moved my grandpappy's pond n the bull frogs never stopped croaking.
- You may be thinkin' yore town am small but our town is so small the town square only has three sides.
- You wanna hear a sad story? Well, my mother-in-law died. But, that ain't sad. She dun drove off a cliff in a truck. And, that ain't the sad part. She drove off the cliff in my brand new truck...and that's why I'm a cryin' !
- I come home the other nite and when I walked thru the door I knowed I wuz in trouble from the funny look my wife give me...yep, my chances with her wuz either 'slim' or 'none' and 'slim' wuz walkin' out the door!
- Our town's Liar's Club held its annual liars competition to see who could tell the biggest lie. It wuz fer amateurs only, no politicians allowed!

Riddle me this!

Everybody likes a good riddle, such as, "They're put on the table, cut and served but never eaten".

What are they?

Why, they's a deck of cards!

Here am some good un's:

1. Can you spell 'butter' in four letters?
2. It can whistle but can't talk...
3. Crooked as a blacksnake, level as a plate, fifty oxen can't pull it straight.
4. My pappy gave it to me, though it belongs to my grampa. Despite my havin' it, my grampa kept it. Although I have it with me at all times, other people use it more that I.
5. Wasn't my sister, wasn't my brother, yet was the child of my pappy and my mammy.
6. Though you use it every day, nobody can sell it to you, nobody can give it to you and when you've got it, you don't know it.
7. Lizzie has it in front, Earl behind, girl once and boy never.

Answers: 1. A goat, 2. The wind, 3. A creek, 4, my name, 5. Me, 6. Sleep, 7. The letter 'L'.

Go to the head of the class!

Here am some questions from one of our tests at the ole' school at Possum Holler. We had to pass this here test to graduate from eighth grade. Let's see how smart you'uns be by takin' it.

The answers am on the next page...no peekin'!

1. How many times can you subtract 2 from 17 ?

2. How far can a dog run into the woods ?

3. Which is heavier, a ton of bricks or a ton of feathers ?

4. How many of each animal did Moses take on the ark ?

5. In what month do people eat the least ?

6. Where does 11 plus 2 equal 1 ?

7. Johnny's mother has three children. One is named 'Penny'. One is named 'Nickel'. What is the third one named?

8. Why do firemen wear red suspenders ?

9. How many days of the week start with the letter 't' ?

10. In the Hawkins family, there are seven sisters. Each sister has one brother. Including Mr. and Mrs. Hawkins, how many are in the family?

Answers:

We hope we didn't catch you a peekin fer you wuz dun!
Here am the answers:

1. You kin only subtract 2 from 21 once. After that you is takin' it away from 19, then 17, and so on.

2. Only halfway, cuz after that it am a runnin' "out of the woods."

3. They both of 'em weighs the same you nincompoop !

4. Trick question...Moses didn't go on the ark, it wuz Noah !

5. Folks eat less in February cuz it am the shortest month.

6. If'n you look at the face of a clock, you will see that 11:00 o'clock plus two is one o'clock.

7. Read that thar question again!

8. To hold thar pants up...what did you think ?

9. Four: Tuesday, Thursday, today and tomorrow.

10. Thar be ten. Each sister has one brother, but they all shares that one brother !

If you got all ten correct: Well hello, Mr. Einstein !
9, 8 or 7: go to the head of the class.
6,5, or 4 : you ain't the sharpest tack in the box.
3, 2, or 1 : Child, you need to go back to school !

A crayon box full of colors:

When we talk 'bout the people of the Appalachian Mountains, we know that includes people of many backgrounds.

Why, thar are still Native Americans of the Cherokee tribe livin' in the Smokey Mountains and members of the Choctaw tribe be a livin' in Alabama.

Folks from Scotland and Ireland weren't the only Europeans to settle in these hills! Davy Crockett's people were French.

Lots of folks here-a-bouts has some English or German blood.

They's also people from Greece, Spain, Italy, Russia, Scandinavia, the Near East and the Far East.

African Americans may have arrived on slave ships but today they is as American as anyone else.

And we can thank our neighbors from South of the Border for all the Mexican restaurants that most every town has.

They's even a Chinese restaurant jes down the street from whar we live!

If'n we wuz to just judge people by the color of thar skin, we would be deprivin' ourselves of knowin' some mighty fine folks.

Maybe we should jes think of these hills as bein' like a big ole' box of crayons what holds every color thar is, and think of how pretty that makes our mountains!

So, be like us n jes smile rite big and say "Howdy!" to everybody you meet!

About the Author

John Leslie Oliver is a man from the foothills of the Appalachian Mountains, where his ancestors first set foot in the early 1700's. An artist, educator, historian, and raconteur, he has collected hill country lore for most of his life and gladly shares it and his sense of humor with all who read this book.

www.ingramcontent.com/pod-product-compliance
Lightning Source LLC
Chambersburg PA
CBHW060404050426
42449CB00009B/1891